My Mom's Deployment

A deployment and reunion
Activity Book
for young children

Elva Resa ✳ Saint Paul

An Elva Resa book

Written by Julie LaBelle ★ Illustrated by Christina Rodriguez

M000017604

★ A note to parents, teachers, and caregivers ★

The activities in this book are meant to help young children express their thoughts and feelings while they have a parent deployed. Not only do these activities reinforce concepts young children are already learning, such as counting, matching, and telling time, they also offer children the opportunity to ask questions, talk about their feelings, and feel connected to their deployed parent.

This activity book is broken into four sections, with activities appropriate for each stage of deployment:

Find a place where you and your child can focus on the activities. Take time to ask your child what he or she is feeling and answer questions in an age-appropriate way. Come back to this book as you enter each stage of deployment, from packing and saying goodbye to welcoming Mom home. This process will help children feel as if they are a part of the process and will help them prepare for what's coming next.

For more about supporting children during deployments, visit SurvivingDeployment.com. Also available: *My Dad's Deployment: A deployment and reunion activity book for young children*.

My Mom's Deployment: A deployment and reunion activity book for young children
Text and illustrations ©2010 Elva Resa Publishing. All rights reserved. No part of this publication may be reproduced without prior written permission of the publisher.

Written by Julie LaBelle for Elva Resa Publishing, except prayer (p. 8) and story (p. 57) written by Alexander Pavlicin.
Illustrated by Christina Rodriguez and Elva Resa staff for Elva Resa Publishing.
Design by Andermax Studios.
Special thanks to our testers: Erin, Alli, Elsa, Sean, Ryan, Ben, and Alexander.

ISBN 978-1-934617-08-3
Printed in United States of America.
 2 3 4 5 6 7 8 9 10

Bulk discounts available.
Elva Resa Publishing
8362 Tamarack Vlg, Ste 119-106, St Paul, MN 55125
ElvaResa.com
MilitaryFamilyBooks.com

Getting Ready for Deployment

What Does "Deploy" Mean?

Deployment means your mom will travel away from home to serve her country and do her job. She might be gone a long time. When she is done with this job, she will come home to you and your family.

Other People Who Have Deployed

Do you know other people who have deployed?
Write down their names and draw their faces.

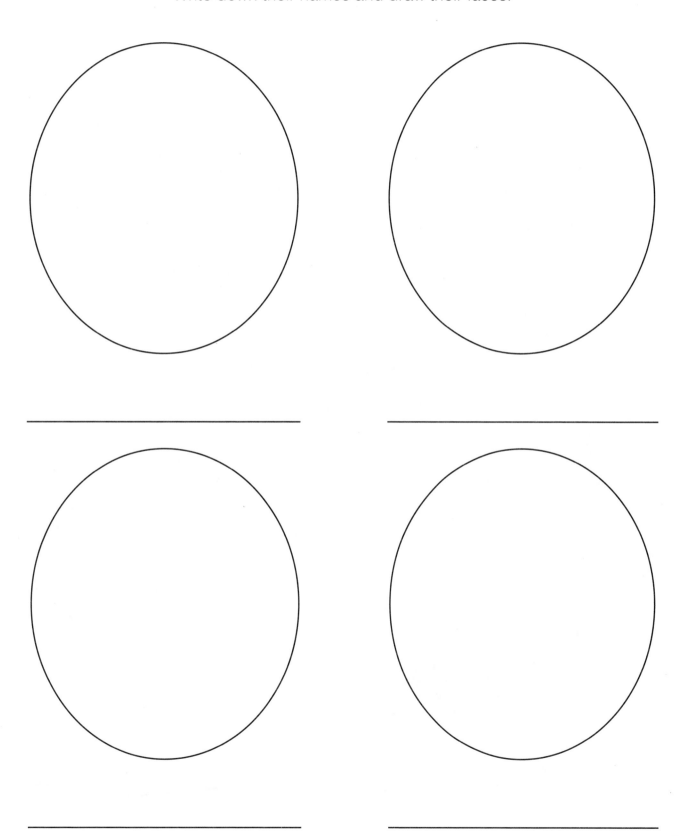

Map of the World

Color the map. Draw a heart where you are.

Draw a heart where your mom will be. Connect the hearts.

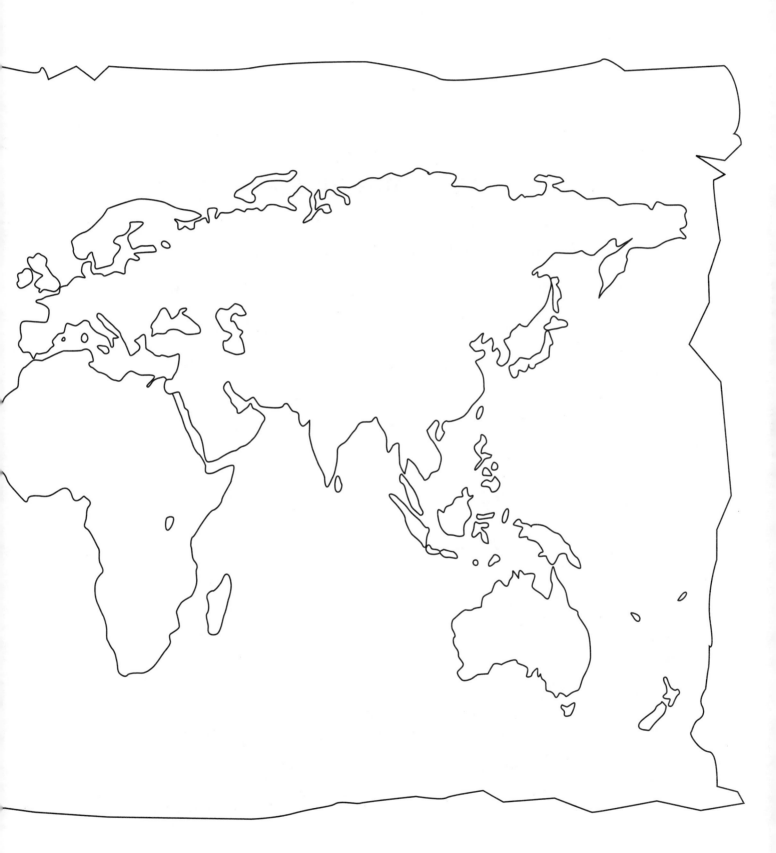

Prayer for Safety

Sometimes it feels like there is nothing you can do to help when someone you love is going away for a while. One thing you can do is say a prayer. You can say this prayer or make up your own prayer.

Dear God,
Please help Mommy stay safe while she is deployed. Help her to come home soon. Watch over our family while Mommy is gone. Please keep Mommy close to us through our prayers and the ways we stay in touch.
                                        Amen.

We Can Stay in Touch

Staying in touch means that even though you cannot see each other in person, you can still do things together and speak to each other. You can still tell each other about your day and say I love you in different ways.

Trace the words.

Circle the ways you can stay in touch with your mom.

Talk on the phone

Send special packages

Write and mail letters

Share photos

Color and mail pictures

Email each other

Things Mom and I Can Do Before She Deploys

Mom has lots of packing to do to get ready for her deployment. You have things you can do with Mom to help you feel ready, too. Color the pictures to show things you and Mom can do together before she deploys.

😊 We can call each other so I can practice talking on the phone.

😊 We can give each other something special. During the deployment we can look at our gifts and think of each other.

😊 We can take a walk together and talk about deployment.

😊 We can talk about ways we can stay in touch.

☺ I can sit on Mom's lap and tell her how I feel.

☺ We can make a project together that will help me remember Mom after she leaves.

More ideas (write them here and draw a picture below) _____

_____

_____

Our Favorite Place

Together draw a picture of a favorite place you like to go together. Color your picture.

Our Favorite Things to Do

Together draw a picture of a favorite thing you like to do together. Color your picture.

We Will Both Sleep Under the Same Moon

We Will Both Wake Up to the Same Sun

Make a Patriotic Mailbox

While Mom is deployed, you will probably send each other cards and letters. This patriotic mailbox will give you a special place to keep letters to and from Mom.

What you will need:

★ Empty shoebox

★ Red, white, and blue colored paper

★ Star stickers

★ Glue stick

★ Scissors

★ Tape

To make your own mailbox:

1. Cover the shoebox with white paper. Cover the lid and bottom separately.
2. Cut a square of blue paper and add star stickers. Attach the square with the stars to the upper left corner of the box lid.
3. Cut seven strips of red paper. Glue to the top of the box to make the flag stripes.
4. Write MAILBOX on the side of your box. Use your mailbox to store letters to and from Mom.

Messages in a Jar

It's nice to get a message from Mom, even on days when she can't write or call. Together, cut out the messages below and put them in a jar. While Mom is deployed, pull out a message at bedtime or whenever you want to hear from her. You and Mom can create your own messages on the extra strips and by cutting up blank paper to write on.

I think of you each day.

Goodnight. I love you!

Did you brush your teeth?

You are my sunshine.

Messages

Deployment Time Capsule

A time capsule is a special place where you can keep important things you want people to see in the future. You can make your own deployment time capsule—all it takes is a box or jar and some things you want your mom to see when she gets home!

You will need:

A shoebox or jar with a lid

Photos

A note to your mom

A list of your favorite things, such as your favorite:

- ☺ Food
- ☺ Movie
- ☺ Book
- ☺ Song
- ☺ Activities
- ☺ Friends
- ☺ TV show
- ☺ Stuffed animal
- ☺ Clothes
- ☺ Toy

Wrapping paper

Tape

To make your capsule:

Inside your box or jar, place your photos, note, and list of favorites. Close the lid and wrap with colored paper. Mark the date on your box or jar, and write "Deployment Time Capsule." When your mom comes home, you can open your time capsule together. You can talk about how things have changed and how they have stayed the same.

Color the Pinwheel

A Few Good Surprises
(Mom – Don't Look!)

When Mom's clothes are packed, ask Dad to help you tuck in a few surprises.

Some ideas:

- ☺ A picture you colored folded into her shirt

- ☺ A laminated picture of you

- ☺ A piece of candy tucked in her pocket

- ☺ Other special things: _____

Ssshhhhhh! Keep it a surprise!

Learn Mom's Alphabet

People in the military use words for different letters of the alphabet. When it is noisy, it is easier to hear words like Alpha, Bravo, and Charlie than A, B, and C. What other words can you think of to go with each letter? Write the word or draw a picture.

A   Alpha

B   Bravo

C   Charlie

D   Delta

E   Echo

F   Foxtrot

G   Golf

H   Hotel

I   India

J   Juliett

K   Kilo

L   Lima

M   Mike

N   November

O   Oscar

P   Papa

Q   Quebec

R   Romeo

S   Sierra

T   Tango

U   Uniform

V   Victor

W   Whiskey

X   X-ray

Y   Yankee

Z   Zulu

Connect the Dots

Connect the Dots

Connect the Dots

Connect the Dots

Connect the Dots

Packing Bags

Help Mom find things she needs to put in her bag for her trip. Find and circle each of the words from the list below. Words may appear forward or backward, horizontally, vertically, or diagonally.

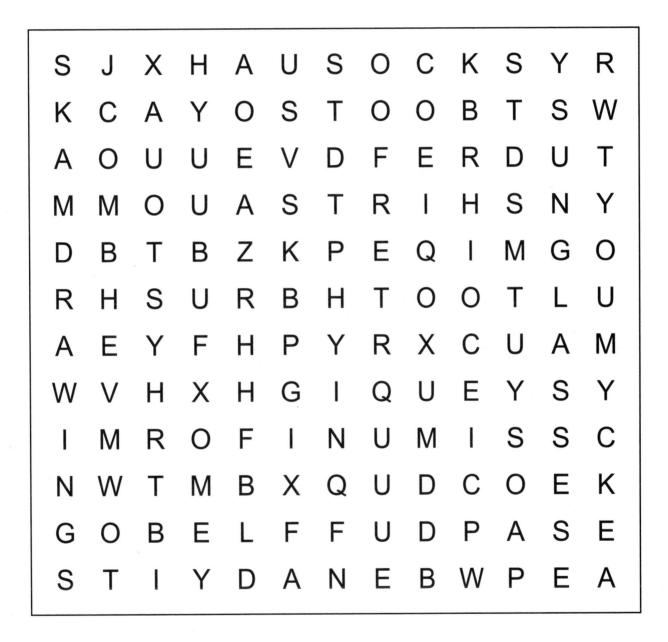

```
S  J  X  H  A  U  S  O  C  K  S  Y  R
K  C  A  Y  O  S  T  O  O  B  T  S  W
A  O  U  U  E  V  D  F  E  R  D  U  T
M  M  O  U  A  S  T  R  I  H  S  N  Y
D  B  T  B  Z  K  P  E  Q  I  M  G  O
R  H  S  U  R  B  H  T  O  O  T  L  U
A  E  Y  F  H  P  Y  R  X  C  U  A  M
W  V  H  X  H  G  I  Q  U  E  Y  S  Y
I  M  R  O  F  I  N  U  M  I  S  S  C
N  W  T  M  B  X  Q  U  D  C  O  E  K
G  O  B  E  L  F  F  U  D  P  A  S  E
S  T  I  Y  D  A  N  E  B  W  P  E  A
```

book	comb	duffle	shirts	socks	toothbush
boots	drawings	photos	soap	sunglasses	uniform

29

On the Day Mom Leaves

Circle the things you might do together when Mom leaves.

Hug

Eat a special meal together

Drive in a car

Hold hands

Say goodbye at home

Say goodbye someplace else

After We Say Goodbye

Circle the things you might do after saying goodbye to Mom.

Take a walk with Dad

Eat ice cream

Play with friends

Snuggle and watch a movie

Give and receive lots of hugs

Draw pictures

What Comes Next?

Draw what comes next in the pattern.

Deployment

Feelings

Circle the face that shows how you feel today about Mom's deployment.

sad

happy

confused

mad

tired

silly

scared

excited

When I Feel Scared

Circle the things you might do when you feel scared.

Tell someone how I feel

Ask for a hug

Keep a flashlight by my bed

Cuddle with someone I love

Say my prayers

Watch a happy movie

Turn on a night light in my room

Read a special book

When I Feel Angry

Circle the things you might do when you feel angry.

Kick a ball outside

Run really fast, back and forth in the yard

Squish a pillow

Sing a favorite song

Clap my hands

Dance around to music

When I Feel Sad

Circle the things you might do when you feel sad.

Cuddle with a special blanket
or stuffed animal

Draw a picture of how I feel

Ask for a hug

Think of a funny joke or story

Ask questions if I don't understand
or I am worried

Play with a good friend
who can cheer me up

Helping Around the House

Make a list of the ways you can help around the house while Mom is away.

☑ Set the table

☐ Help fold clothes

☐ Make my bed

☐ Pick up toys

☐ _____

☐ _____

When Mom Calls

Think about what you would like to say to Mom if she calls on the phone.
You can practice on a toy phone.

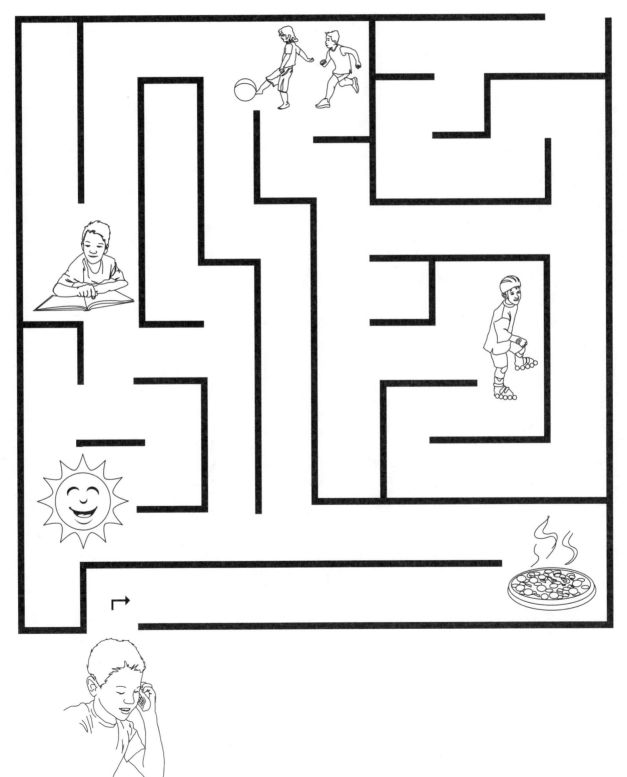

Wishing Trees

Even on the days when you can't talk to Mom on the phone or send emails, you can still wish good things for her. On a wishing tree, you write a wish or prayer and attach it to the tree. There are many ways to make a wishing tree. Here is one way:

What you will need:

★ Large piece of construction paper or poster board
★ Colored paper
★ Crayons or markers
★ Glue stick
★ Scissors

To make your wishing tree:

1. Draw a tree on the large piece of paper or poster board.
2. Using the colored paper, cut out shapes of hearts, stars, leaves, or ribbons.
3. Write a wish or prayer for Mom on each shape you cut out.
4. Glue the wishes onto your tree.
5. Hang your wishing tree in your room, on the refrigerator, or another special place where you can see your wishes and add more whenever you want to.

For more wishing tree ideas, go to ElvaResa.com/wishingtree.html

Make a Wish!

Color the wishing tree, then write a special wish on the ribbon at the bottom.

Based on the book *The Wishing Tree* by Mary Redman and Christina Rodriguez. ElvaResa.com/book/wishing-tree/

Some Things Stay the Same; Some Are Different

When Mom is away, some things change, but other things stay the same. Write the words or draw a picture to describe what you do when Mom is home and what you do when she is deployed.

When Mom is home:

We eat _____.

We go to bed at _____.

We play _____.

We _____ on Saturday mornings.

When Mom is deployed:

We eat _____.

We go to bed at _____.

We play _____.

We _____ on Saturday mornings.

What stays the same? What is different?

Some Things Stay the Same; Some Are Different

Color all the things you can do when Mom is home.
Circle the things you still can do when Mom is deployed.

Eat pizza

Read books

Go to the park

Wrestle with Dad

Watch a movie

Do a puzzle

Play a game

Snuggle

What stays the same? What is different?

Scavenger Hunt

Hunt for these items to send in your next care package to Mom. Check the box when you find the item.

❏ A picture of me

❏ A story I made up

❏ A leaf or flower from the yard

❏ A picture I drew

❏ A sticker

❏ A special treat

Messages From Home

Tear out this page and ask your friends and family to write special messages on the back to send to Mom. Have them sign their names. You may need to use more sheets of paper for all your messages. Decorate your pages and send them to Mom.

Messages From Home

Messages From Mom and Her Friends

Tear out this page and mail it to Mom. Ask her to collect autographs and messages from her friends and send them back to you.

Messages From Mom and Her Friends

Photo Collage of Mom and Her Friends

When someone is away for a long time, it is nice to have lots of pictures around to remind us of what the person looks like and what we love about the person. While Mom is deployed, you can create a special poster of Mom and some of the people she works with.

What you will need:

★ Pictures of Mom and her friends

★ Poster board

★ Glue stick

★ Markers and stickers

To make your poster:

1. Ask Mom to send you pictures of herself and her friends.

2. Decorate the border of the poster board using stickers and markers.

3. Glue pictures of Mom and her friends to the poster board.

4. Hang your collage on the wall for your family and friends to see.

A Picture of Me

Draw and color a picture of yourself. Remember to add hair, eyes, and the clothes you like to wear. You can send your picture to Mom or show it to her when she comes home.

_____
(Sign your name)

My Hand

Trace your hand below. Color or paint your hand drawing. Decorate it with rings, fingernails, bracelets, or a watch. You can send your hand picture to Mom or show it to her when she comes home.

Time Difference

Around the world, we have different time zones. For example, when it is 9:00 a.m. in California, it is 12:00 p.m. in New York, and it is 5:00 p.m. in England. You and your mom both eat and sleep, but do you do it at the same time? With an adult, figure out the difference in time between where you live and where Mom is deployed.

At home the time is: Where Mom is, the time is:

morning

lunch time

afternoon

dinner time

night

Time Difference

Draw a line to show what Mom is doing while you are waking up, eating lunch, playing with friends, eating dinner, and sleeping.

When I am: Mom is:

Learning About Where Mom Is Deployed

Find out more about where your mom is deployed. Ask an adult to help you find out the answers to these questions:

My mom is deployed to _____(base/city)_____ , which is in

_____(country)_____ . The people there speak _____(language)_____ ,

and this is how they say "hello": _____ . Many people there really like

to _____(an activity)_____ . The weather there is _____(hot/cold)_____ ,

so Mom needs lots of _____(item of clothing)_____ .

This is the most interesting thing I learned about where Mom is deployed:

_____

_____

_____

_____

_____

What Does It Look Like There?

What does it look like where Mom is deployed? Ask Mom to send you pictures or with an adult go to the library or to a website to see pictures of the military base, city, or country where Mom is deployed. What is the same or different from where you live?

Draw a picture of what you think it looks like where Mom is:

★ ★ ★ ★ ★ ★ ★ ★ ★ ★ ★ ★ ★ ★ ★

★ ★ ★ ★ ★ ★ ★ ★ ★ ★ ★ ★ ★ ★ ★

What Does Mom Do at Work?

Color the pictures to show what Mom might do today at work.

Fly an airplane

Eat lunch

Ride in a helicopter

Sleep in a tent

March in formation

Read a letter

Drive a truck

Think about me!

Goofy Story

Fill in a word for each question.

1. A food I like to eat: _____

2. An interesting color: _____

3. How I feel today: _____

4. My favorite animal: _____

5. Something I do in the morning: _____

6. A strange noise: _____

7. A friend's name: _____

8. What I say when it's time for a bath: _____

Now match the word for each numbered question above to the numbered lines below to create a goofy story.

One day, I was _____(5)_____ with my _____(4)_____ when I

heard a loud _____(6)_____. I looked up and saw a giant bucket of

_____(2)_____ _____(1)_____. My _____(4)_____

started eating the _____(2)_____ _____(1)_____ so my friend

_____(7)_____ shouted "_____(8)_____." And that is why I am

feeling _____(3)_____ today.

Things I Am Learning To Do

Everyone learns new things during a deployment. With an adult, keep track of some of the things you are learning during your mom's deployment.

☐ I can count to _____
(date)

1 2 ³ 4 5

☐ I can spell my name _____
(date)

☐ I can tie my shoes _____
(date)

☐ I know my address _____

_____
(date)

☐ I know my phone number _____
(date)

☐ I know my ABCs _____
(date)

A B C

☐ I can zip a zipper _____
(date)

☐ I can button a button _____
(date)

Other things I am learning to do:

Learning to Spell and Write

Mom   Mom   Mom   Mom

Dad   Dad   Dad   Dad

I Love You   I Love You

Aa Bb Cc Dd Ee Ff Gg

Hh Ii Jj Kk Ll Mm Nn Oo

Pp Qq Rr Ss Tt Uu Vv

Ww Xx Yy Zz

(my name)

My Favorite Things

Sometimes our favorite things change over time. What are your favorites today?

Food:

Books:

Activities:

Friends:

Songs:

Movie or TV show:

Look at Me Grow!

With a grownup, make a growth chart to keep track of how much you grow while Mom is away.

You will need:

★ 5 sheets of cardstock or paper
★ Tape
★ Marker
★ Ruler
★ Stickers

How to make your growth chart:

1. Tape the pieces of paper together, end to end, until it is taller than you are.

2. Hang the chart on the wall.

3. Ask Dad or another adult to mark the paper in inches and feet, measuring from the floor up the wall.

4. Every month ask someone to mark your height. Stand up straight with your feet flat on the floor and your heels to the wall. Look straight ahead.

5. Be sure to write the date next to your height marker.

You can show Mom how much you've grown when she comes home!

Or, you can ask Dad to take a picture of you in the same spot every month. Look at the pictures with Mom when she gets home so she can see how much you've grown.

Hugs Hugs Hugs

Hugs are wonderful! Who can you hug today?

My Little Book of Mom

Color the pictures and cut them apart. Then staple the pictures together in any order and use them to tell a story about your mom.

Book of Mom

My Little Book of Symbols

Color the pictures, then cut them apart and staple together in the order you want for your book. Talk with a friend about what each of the symbols means to you.

Book of Symbols

Getting Ready for Reunion

Things I Want to Do When Mom Comes Home

Circle the things you would like to do with Mom when she comes home.

Hug

Read a book

Eat ice cream

Cuddle

Get tucked in bed

Sing a happy song

Go for a walk

Eat our favorite meal together

Mom and Me Finger Puppets

You'll need a washable marker and two fingers. With an adult's help, draw Mom's face on one finger and your face on the other finger. Now you and your little finger puppets can talk to each other. Pretend you are talking to Mom when she comes home. What would your puppets say to each other?

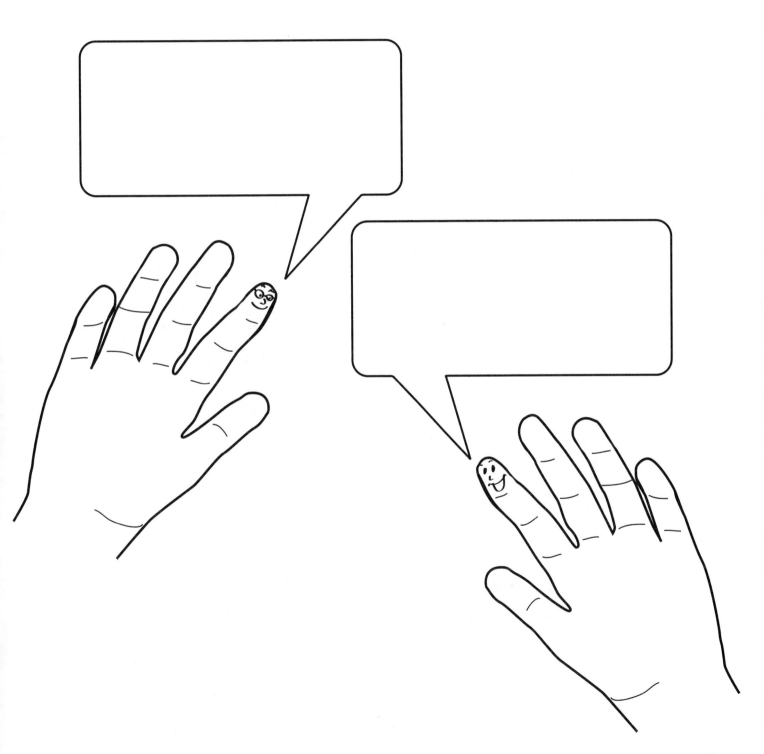

Ways to Welcome Mom Home

Color the pictures to show ways you would like to welcome Mom home.

Fly the American flag.

Make a giant poster with
"Welcome Home Mommy!" on it.

Tie yellow ribbons around the house and yard.

Make some of Mom's favorite foods.

Get out Mom's favorite game to play.

Pick up my room and toys. Help Dad get the house ready.

Welcome Home Card

Make Mom a welcome home card.

You will need:

★ Paper

★ Stickers

★ Crayons or markers

★ Your creativity!

To make your card:

1. Fold your piece of paper in half.

2. On the front of the card, draw and color a picture or write "Welcome Home."

3. On the inside, write a note or draw a picture for Mom. Sign your name.

4. Put your card in a special place to give to Mom when she comes home.

Welcome Home Poster

Make Mom a welcome home poster.

You will need:

★ Poster board

★ Markers or crayons

★ Stickers

★ Balloons (optional)

To make your poster:

1. Ask an adult to help you write a big welcome home message on your poster.

2. Color your poster and add pictures and stickers.

3. Blow up the balloons and tape them to the corners of your poster.

4. Hang the poster where Mom will see it and give her a great big welcome!

Sidewalk Chalk Welcome Home Sign

Make a sidewalk chalk sign to welcome Mom home.

What you will need:

★ Colored chalk

★ A sidewalk or driveway

★ An adult to help

★ A camera (optional)

To make your sidewalk chalk sign:

1. With an adult, find a safe place on the sidewalk or driveway where you can use your chalk to draw.

2. Draw pictures and write "Welcome Home" using your chalk.

3. When Mom comes home, show her your masterpiece!

4. If it might rain before Mom will see your sidewalk chalk sign, take a picture to show her later.

Paper Loop Chain Decoration

Decorate for homecoming with a red, white, and blue paper loop chain.

You will need:

★ 9 sheets of construction paper (3 red, 3 white, and 3 blue)

★ Ruler

★ Tape or stapler

★ Scissors

To make your paper loop chain:

1. Cut your paper into strips.

2. Loop a red strip into a circle and ask an adult to help you tape or staple the ends together.

3. Loop a white strip through the first red loop and tape or staple the ends.

4. Loop a blue strip through the white loop and tape or staple the ends.

5. Continue your red, white, and blue pattern until you've used up all the strips.

6. Decorate your front door or another special place with your chain.

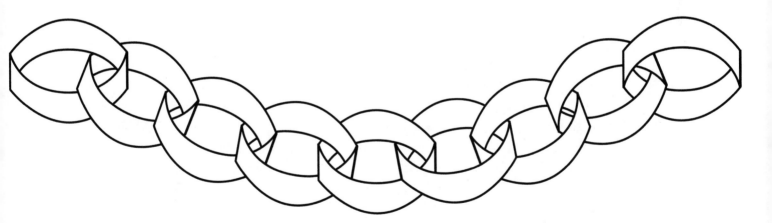

Match and Rhyme

Match the words that rhyme.

salute

plane

guitar

tent

flag

star

bag

rain

boot

cent

How Many?

Draw a line from the number on the left to the number of objects that match it.

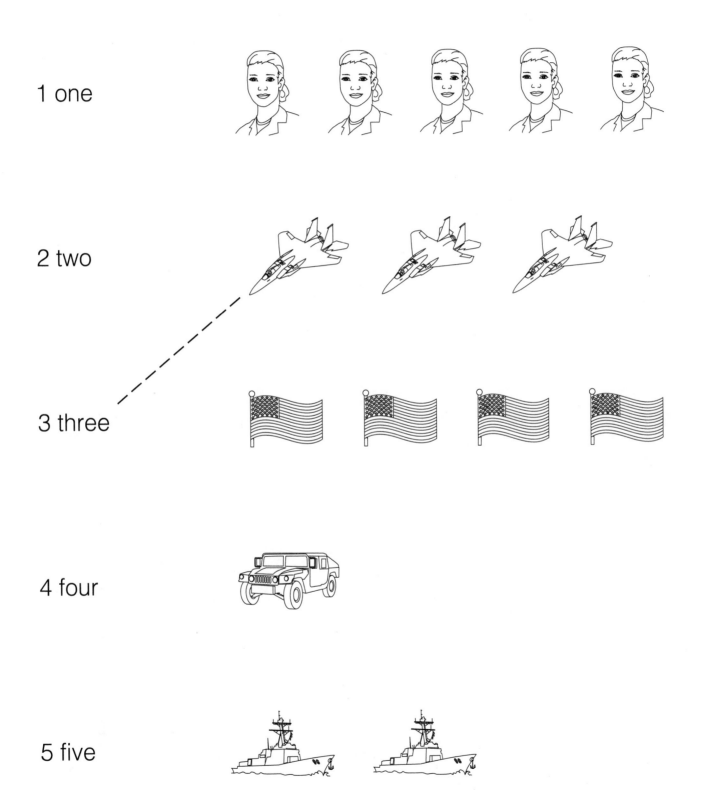

What Does Not Belong?

Circle the item in each row that does not belong with the others.

Matching

Draw a line from the item on the left to the object on the right it goes with.

I'm Proud of My Mom

There are lots of reasons to be proud of your mom. Think of some of the reasons you are proud of her. Then draw a picture of your mom and tell why you are most proud.

- My mom is strong.
- My mom is kind.
- My mom protects America.
- My mom is my hero.
- My mom teaches me things.

- My mom is brave.
- My mom is smart.
- My mom protects me and my family.
- My mom takes care of us.
- My mom is my best buddy.

I am most proud of my mom because:

This is a picture of my mom:

What Kind of Hugs?

On homecoming day, what kind of hugs would you like best? Circle all the kinds of hugs you would like to give or receive.

How I Feel

Circle the faces that show how you might feel on homecoming day.

How Will Mom Get Home?

Circle the ways Mom will travel to get home.

What Should I Wear?

Pick out the clothes you want to wear on homecoming day. Color the clothes you think would make a nice outfit to wear when you welcome Mom home.

Ways I Have Changed

You've grown while Mom was gone. What else about you has changed since Mom deployed? Draw two pictures, one that shows you before Mom deployed and one that shows you now.

Before Mom deployed	Now

How Might Mom Be Different?

Just as you have changed while Mom's been gone, some things about Mom might have changed, too. Talk with an adult about the ways you think Mom might be different.

She might:

- ★ have a tan
- ★ like new foods
- ★ have new friends

- ★ want to be quiet sometimes
- ★ feel a little grumpy and tired
- ★ know new things

Draw a picture of how you think Mom might be different when she comes home.

Which Is the Biggest?

Circle which one is bigger in each row.

Reunion

Help Mom Find Her Way Home

Draw a line from Mom to you to help her find her way home.

Help Mom and Dad Find Each Other

Draw a line from Mom to Dad
so they can give each other a big hug and kiss!

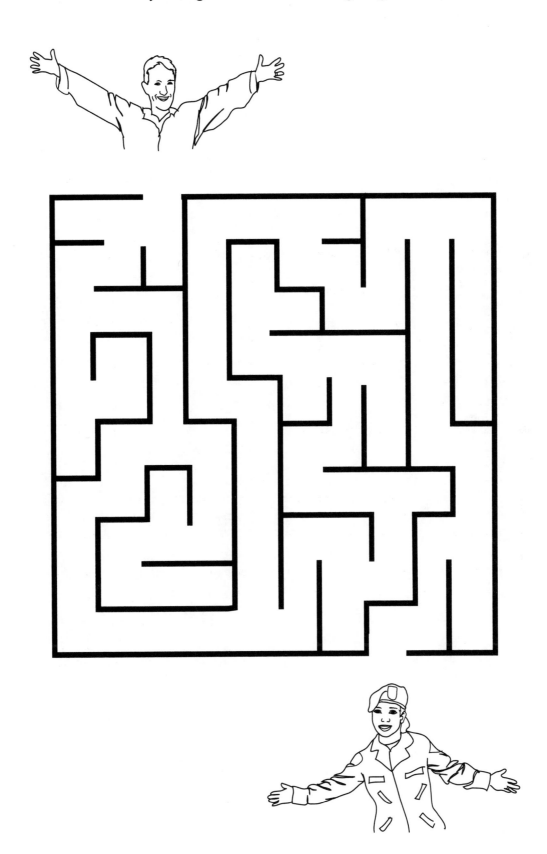

Things We'll Do on Homecoming Day

Circle the things you will do the day Mom comes home.

Wash my face

Brush my teeth

Comb my hair

Make my bed

Put on my special clothes

Get ready for big hugs!

A Picture of Mom and Me on the Day She Comes Home

Draw a picture or glue a photo of you and Mom in the frame.

Ways I Can Help Mom Feel Welcome at Home

Color the pictures and circle the ways you can help Mom feel welcome.

Get her favorite pajamas and slippers ready

Tell her how much I love her

Ask her to play games

Let Mom rest and get used to being home

Let Mom and Dad spend
some quiet time together

American Flag

Color the American flag by matching the numbers to the correct colors.

1=Red
2=White
3=Blue

Match the Hugs

Color the pictures and circle the two that match.

More Things to Do With Mom

Circle the things you want to do with Mom now that she is home. Color the pictures.

Sing a favorite song

Eat a favorite food

Read a favorite book

Watch a favorite movie

Play a favorite game

Go to a favorite park

Sharing With Mom

When Mom comes home everyone will need to share.
Circle the things you will share.

How Many?

Color the correct number in each row.

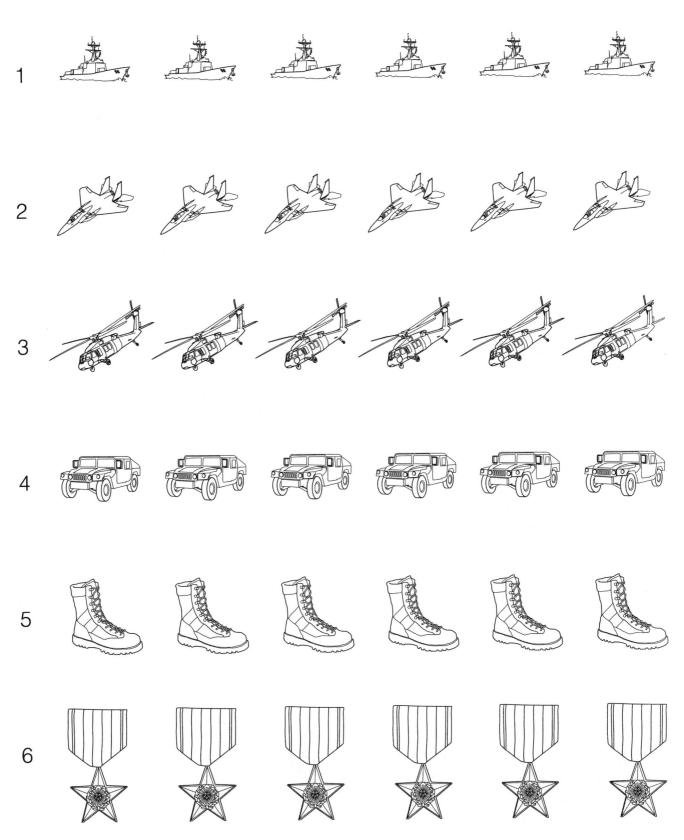

1

2

3

4

5

6

Color-By-Number

Color the picture by matching the numbers to the colors listed below.

1=green
2=yellow
3=blue
4=red

God Bless America

Color the picture.

Matching

Color the two planes that are the same.

Matching

Color the two ships that match.

Mom's Story

Ask Mom to tell you a story about her deployment.

Draw a picture about Mom's story.

What I Can Do Now

Share with Mom the new skills you learned while she was gone.

Hidden Picture

Find the hidden flag. Color the picture.

Open the Deployment Capsule

It's time to open your deployment time capsule with Mom! Gather your family around and open your time capsule. Look at the things you put in your box or jar.

Are you different now than when you started your time capsule? How have things changed? What stayed the same?

Things Our Family Learned Together

There are many things your family might have learned during Mom's deployment.

★ To be brave and help each other.

★ To rely on each other and ask each other for help.

★ To be patient and kind.

★ To stay in touch.

★ To give great hugs!

Draw a picture to show some of the things your family learned during Mom's deployment.

We Are Thankful

Draw pictures of some of the things you and your family are thankful for now that the deployment is over.

You Did It!

Draw a picture of your favorite part of this deployment.

Draw a picture of your least favorite part of this deployment.

CERTIFICATE OF ACHIEVEMENT

Awarded to:

_____

For learning so much during Mom's deployment to _____

and for being an all-around great kid!

GREAT
JOB!

Awarded by:

_____

Awarded on:

_____